School is fun—I like to learn,
and I work hard all day.
When Friday comes,
I'm happy, Lord,
and so I shout, "Hooray!"

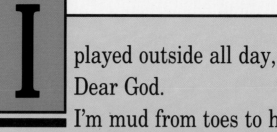

I played outside all day,
Dear God.
I'm mud from toes to head.
I think I'd like to take a
bath before I go to bed.

I love to sing when I'm alone,
and with my best friend, too.
If you will listen now,
Dear God,
I'll sing a song for you.

Dear God, I want to
go to church
so I can see my friends.
We sing and talk
about your love.
It never, ever ends.

Dear God,

I'm glad we're all together

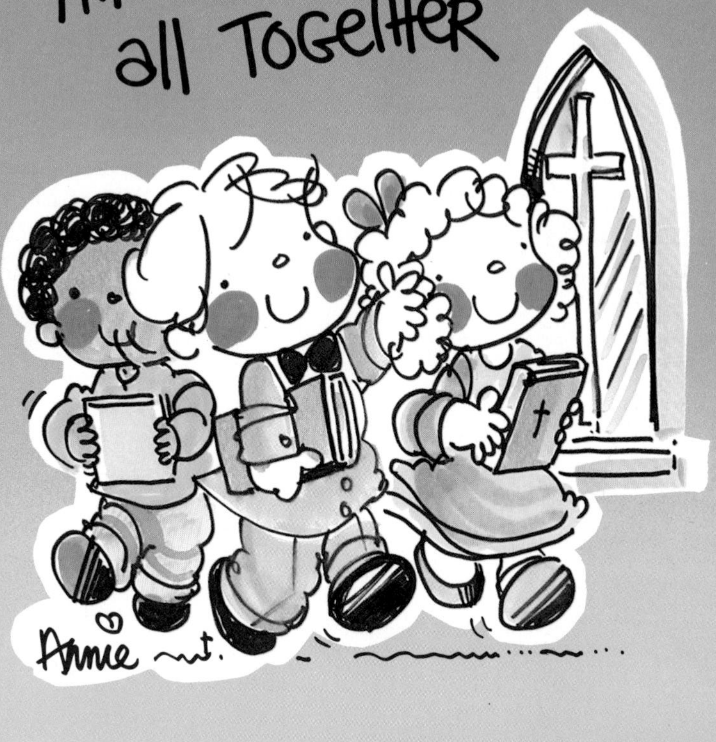

My eyes are pretty—
so's my hair.
That's not so hard to see.
You knew what you
were doing, Lord,
when you created me.

Dear God,
you made me,
... so I guess I'm OK

Annie

Sometimes I make mistakes,
Dear God.
I'm sorry, but I do.
But I can always start again
on something that's
brand-new.

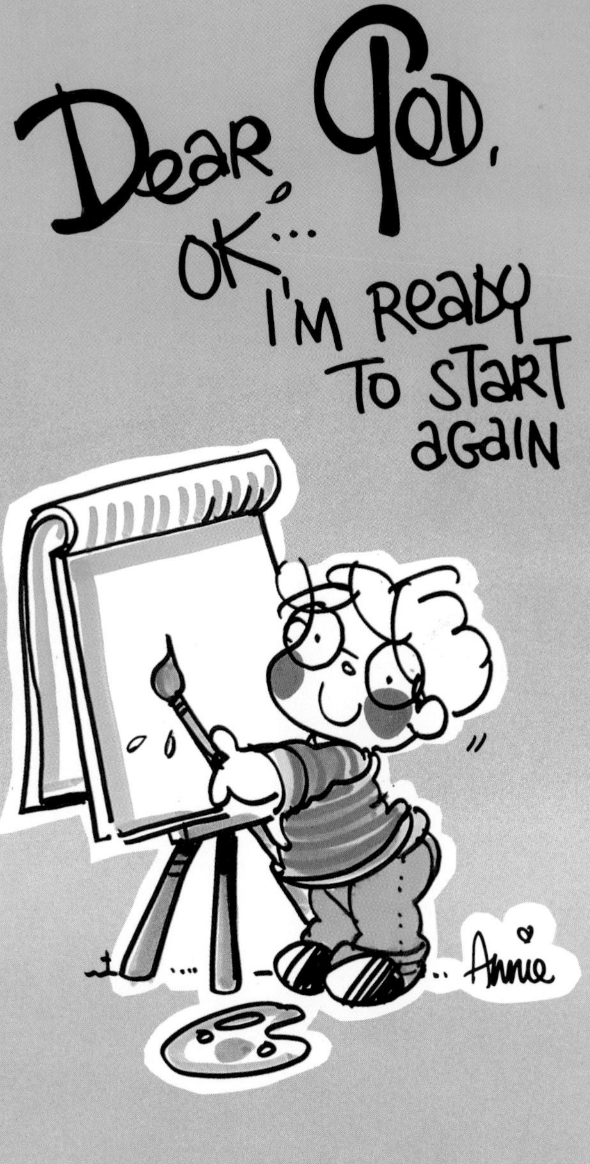
Dear God,
OK...
I'm ready
to start
again
Annie

I love to giggle,
smile, and laugh
'cause laughing feels so good.
I'd like to laugh
and laugh all day.
Dear God, I really would!